INDONESIA

UZON

PHILIPPINES

*Pacific
Ocean*

MINDANAO

SULAWESI

MOLUCCAS

CERAM

IRIAN JAYA

N   E   S   I   A

UMBAWA

FLORES   TIMOR

UMBA

IMAGES OF ASIA

Javanese Gamelan

Titles in the series

Javanese Gamelan
Traditional Orchestra of Indonesia
Second Edition

JENNIFER LINDSAY

SINGAPORE
OXFORD UNIVERSITY PRESS
OXFORD NEW YORK
1992

Oxford University Press

Oxford New York Toronto
Delhi Bombay Calcutta Madras Karachi
Kuala Lumpur Singapore Hong Kong Tokyo
Nairobi Dar es Salaam Cape Town
Melbourne Auckland
and associated companies in
Berlin Ibadan

Oxford is a trade mark of Oxford University Press

© *Oxford University Press Pte. Ltd. 1979, 1992*

First published 1979
Second edition 1992

Published in the United States by
Oxford University Press Inc., New York

ISBN 0 19 588582 1

British Library Cataloguing-in-Publication Data

A catalogue record for this book is available
from the British Library

Library of Congress Cataloging-in-Publication Data

Lindsay, Jennifer.
Javanese gamelan: traditional orchestra of Indonesia / Jennifer
Lindsay.
p.   cm. — *(Images of Asia)*
Includes bibliographical references.
Discography: p.
ISBN 0-19-588582-1 (hard cover):
1. Gamelan.   2. Music — Indonesia — Java — History and criticism.
I. Title.   II. Series.
ML 1251.I53L56   1992
784.2'09598'2 — dc20
92-163
CIP
MN

Printed in Singapore by Kyodo Printing Co. (S) Pte. Ltd.
Published by Oxford University Press Pte. Ltd.,
Unit 221, Ubi Avenue 4, Singapore 1440

Preface

WHEN I first wrote this book in 1979, I certainly did not expect to write a Preface to a revised edition well over a decade later. The book was written originally as an initial guide to Javanese gamelan music for tourists travelling to Java and wishing to make some sense of the 'exotic' sounds that they heard. However, the fact remains that even now there are still few other books that give an introductory explanation of Javanese gamelan. As a result, this book has served a wider purpose than that for which it was originally intended. Most writing on Javanese gamelan is academic discussion that is inaccessible and incomprehensible to those who have had no previous contact with the music. Therefore, not only tourists to Java, but also students of world music and Indonesian studies have few other sources of simple introductory information.

For this reason, I agreed to the publication of *Javanese Gamelan* in a revised edition. Clearly, one's own ideas and perceptions change over time, and if I were to start afresh, I would probably write a very different kind of book. In another sense, however, the more one studies gamelan, the more difficult it is to step back and write simply about its complex musical concepts. The framework of this book, written fifteen years ago, has therefore basically been retained, but the sections describing the structure of gamelan music (Chapter 4) and gamelan's interrelationship with other art forms (Chapter 5) have been expanded. I have chosen to include more detail and to cover briefly some important musical concepts not covered in the first edition. However, as this book is not directed towards the specialist reader, and as there is no aural aid, such as a cassette tape, to give aural illustration to the written examples, the musical explanations are still kept as concise as possible.

Perhaps because it takes a kind of 'freshness' to the subject to explain it in introductory terms to those others who are at a starting-point, there has as yet been no real introductory book on Javanese gamelan written by a Javanese. I hope that this will change and that Javanese musicians will be encouraged to write non-academic books about their music, but meantime this book remains a book written by one outsider for other outsiders. My only qualification for writing this book was that I came to gamelan music initially as untutored as any other visitor to Java and can understand the difficulty visitors face when they hear the music for the first time and wish to make some sense of it.

In the fifteen years since this book was first written, there have been many changes in the situation of Javanese gamelan. Many of the older master musicians who studied and performed in the courts in the colonial times have died. Two of these were my teachers, the late R. Ng. Martopangrawit from Solo and the late R. L. Pustakamardawa (Sastrapustaka) from Yogyakarta. My personal debt to these two teachers extends well beyond their patient teaching of Javanese gamelan. Together with their other students, I feel their loss keenly.

Other friends in Java who have helped me with this book or who have influenced my ideas are too numerous to name. It is indeed their friendship that has drawn me back over the years to Java and to the study of Javanese culture.

For this revised edition, I would like to thank Alan Feinstein who offered valuable editorial suggestions and Joan Suyenaga who generously assisted the photographer, Tara Sosrowardoyo, in arranging photographic sessions.

Jakarta　　　　　　　　　　　　　JENNIFER LINDSAY
July 1991

All photographs except those on pages 5 and 6 are by Tara Sosrowardoyo. Those on the aforementioned pages are by Yazir Marzuki.

Contents

I
The Historical Background

BENEATH the emblem of the Republic of Indonesia is an inscription of an Old Javanese proverb, 'Bhinneka Tunggal Ika', meaning 'Unity in Diversity'. It is a fitting reuse of the proverb, for Indonesia is a nation made up of more than 13,000 islands and hundreds of distinct cultural groups.

One of Indonesia's oldest living cultures and that shared by the majority of its population is that of central Java, an area covering a little more than a third of the island of Java. The population of the province of central Java is 30 million and its population density is among the highest in the world, in some places reaching 2,000 people per square kilometre.

The people who live in central Java are distinct culturally from those who live in the western or eastern parts of the island. While there is considerable blurring at the boundaries, the distinctions are evident initially in terms of language. The language of central Java is Javanese, which is linguistically complex with an intricate system of levels used to define and reflect social status. The heartland of central Javanese culture is generally considered to be the court cities of Surakarta (also known as Solo) and Yogyakarta, where the mastery of Javanese language and accompanying social behaviour is seen to be the most 'correct'. It is here in Surakarta and Yogyakarta, in the area of the eighth-century Mataram kingdom, that the courtly arts of dance, poetry, gamelan, and *wayang kulit* (shadow puppet theatre) developed as distinctly central Javanese arts, but are now known generally without any qualifying term as merely 'Javanese'.

As one moves from central Java towards the west, one finds different Javanese accents, slightly different vocabulary, and parallel variations in music, dance, and *wayang*. To the far west, however, with Bandung as its centre, the language

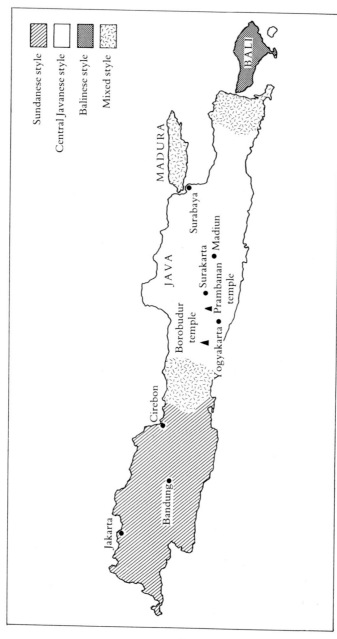

Figure 1. Map of Java and Bali showing the main areas of gamelan development.

Sundanese style
Central Javanese style
Balinese style
Mixed style

BALI

MADURA

Surabaya

JAVA

Surakarta
Madiun
Prambanan
temple

Borobudur
temple
Yogyakarta

Cirebon

Bandung

Jakarta

changes entirely to Sundanese and the gamelan music, the dance, and the theatre have forms of their own.

East of central Java, the variants in Javanese language, dance, and music spread almost to the eastern coast, where one finds cultural forms that appear to combine Javanese and Balinese forms. The language at the far eastern tip of Java, which looks across the strait to Bali, is quite different from either Javanese or Balinese.

Within central Java there is a clear contrast between the type of language, aesthetics, and cultural forms of the inland court cities of Yogyakarta and Surakarta, and those of the northern coast. For centuries the northern coastal cities, which were the gateway for Islam to Java from the fourteenth century onwards, have been more directly linked to the international world of trade. In contrast, the inland courts of Yogyakarta and Surakarta were virtually sheltered from change by the Dutch colonial government, which in giving them special status as semi-independent principalities, allowed the courts the opportunity to develop their arts. Between the contrast of cultural forms from the northern coastal cities and the inland courts, there is a wide spectrum of styles of Javanese music, dance, and theatre which all continue as living traditions, changing in their own ways.

The wealth of art forms of central Java has been forged through a centuries-long process of interaction with each other and with diverse foreign cultures, uniquely blending together aspects from all of them.

The land of Java is one of the oldest continuously populated areas in the world. The Stone Age civilization of Java gave way to the Bronze-Iron Age around the first century AD, brought by the latest migrations from the Asian mainland. Later, traders and merchants from India came to Java, and as this contact increased, so did Hindu culture and religion spread throughout the land.

The influence of India in Java was consolidated over the fifth to seventh centuries by scholars and priests who came to Java and brought with them the refinements of Indian culture: Sanskrit language and script, the *Mahabharata* and *Ramayana*

3

epics, music, dance, and, most importantly, Hindu and Buddhist thought and philosophy. Two of the world's greatest Buddhist and Hindu monuments stand in central Java as testimony to the great flowering of Hindu–Buddhist civilization in Java, namely, the Borobudur and Prambanan temples, built only a century apart in the eighth and ninth centuries.

When Islam appeared in Java in the fourteenth century, brought by Arab traders, its influence spread quickly, although unevenly. Hindu–Buddhism was discarded in favour of Islam. But any visitor to central Java today can still sense the stronger influence of Islamic culture on the northern coast, and will also be struck by the vitality of Hindu-influenced cultural expression in inland central Java. The Hindu legacy runs very deep. Javanese epics are first and foremost those of the *Mahabharata* and *Ramayana*. It is stories from both these epics and the philosophies they espouse that are performed in the Javanese *wayang* or shadow puppet repertoire. The gods and heroes of Javanese mythology are Hindu, and while not worshipped as gods, they serve as models for the Javanese and are figures utterly familiar to most Javanese today.

Central Javanese gamelan music has a unique place in this historical process. While all other aspects of culture in Java at some stage adopted and modified the basic material of Indian culture, gamelan seems to have remained more impervious. The reliefs on the Borobudur and Prambanan temples, for example, show almost exclusively instruments of Indian origin, such as side-blown flutes, bottle-shaped drums, and plucked string instruments which have not survived in Java. Yet, Javanese tradition claims that gamelan music existed long before Prambanan or Borobudur, although the same tradition attributes the creation of gamelan instruments to Hindu gods.

In the beginning, it is said, the god Sang Hyang Guru ruled as king of all Java in his palace at the summit of Maendra mountain in Medangkamulan. This mountain, now called Mount Lawu (near Surakarta in central Java), marked the boundary between the kingdoms of Surakarta and Madiun. The god Guru needed a signal by which he could summon all

1. Relief from Borobudur temple showing side-blown flutes.

2. Relief from Borobudur temple showing a plucked lute.

3. Relief from Borobudur temple showing a percussion instrument.

the gods together, so he made a gong tuned to a certain pitch. As the different messages beaten on the gong became more complicated, he made a second gong tuned to another pitch. In time, he made a third to simplify matters still further, and these three gongs tuned to three different tones formed the original gamelan set named Lokanata or Lokananta (literally, 'King of the World').

Apart from the three gongs, the original gamelan Lokananta is said to have had four other types of percussion instruments: a hand-beaten drum, a *ketuk*, a *kenong*, and a *kemanak*.

What did this ancient music sound like? We are told that the melodies were based on the melodic patterns of the Old Javanese poems called *kidung*. This explanation, together with the account of the creation of gamelan, suggests that there were two kinds of gamelan music. On the one hand, we are told that the three-toned gamelan was for 'giving signals' which became 'more complicated', so we can presume the music was loud and consisted of different complex patterns. On the other hand, the

6

mention of both singing and instruments like *ketuk*, *kenong*, and *kemanak*, suggests another style.

If we understand *ketuk* and *kenong* to be similar in type and function to their modern namesakes, we can interpret them as small horizontal gongs, whose function is to mark phrases. The *kemanak* is a small hand-held instrument made of bronze that has been described by Jaap Kunst as looking like 'a banana with a stalk, opened up along its convex side, with the pulp taken out'. *Kemanak* are played as a pair and have two different tones. Their function is more as a time-keeper, and they are still used for the old and sacred Javanese court dance called *bedaya* when, together with only *gong*, *ketuk*, and *kenong*, they accompany the sung choral accompaniment to the dance.

Javanese explanations for the beginning of gamelan therefore seem to stress that there were two different styles: one style loud, majestic, and possibly only instrumental, which emphasized the actual physical sound of the instruments themselves; the other more soft, with strong ties to the melodic contours of Javanese poetry (which is always sung), in which the function of the instruments is really to organize rhythmically the poetic forms.

Existing old styles of gamelan performance also indicate that a clear division into loud and soft styles remained an important characteristic of Javanese gamelan. Housed in the *kraton* or palaces of Yogyakarta and Surakarta are the oldest existing gamelan sets of the loud style. Each court has two sets tuned to an archaic three-tone scale, the sets of instruments popularly called Gamelan Kodokngorek and Gamelan Munggang, after the names of the pieces of music played on them. These gamelan sets are said to date from the twelfth century and to have been each divided into two parts upon the division of the Mataram kingdom into Yogyakarta and Surakarta in 1755. Neither of these gamelan sets has any of the softer elaborating instruments found in a modern gamelan set, and the music played on them does not use singing. Some of the instruments found in the Kodokngorek and Munggang gamelans, such as the bell-tree (*byong*) and the small cymbals (*rojeh*), are no longer used in modern Javanese ensembles. These old gamelans are also remarkable for their number of large gongs (the Kodok-ngorek gamelan in Yogyakarta has four) and their size. The gong in the Munggang gamelan in Surakarta is over 125 centimetres wide and needs to be hit very hard in order to sound. This is not easy as the hammer weighs 12 kilograms!

The Yogyakarta and Surakarta palaces also house the ancient Sekaten gamelans, which are carried in procession outside the palaces and are played once a year to commemorate the birth of the Prophet Muhammad. Each palace has a pair of Sekaten gamelan, the most ancient set of each pair said to date from the sixteenth century. There is also a Sekaten gamelan in Cirebon, on the north coast of Java, and in earlier times they existed in Madura and Banten. The Sekaten gamelans are tuned to the *pelog* scale and are extremely low in pitch. The *saron* keys are extremely thick and they are hit with very large, heavy buffalo-horn hammers. There is no drum in this ensemble. The orchestra is led by the *bonang*, which is much larger than its modern namesake, and it plays long, solemn solo patterns which lead the whole orchestra in its majestic, loud tone.

While this loud style of gamelan developed particularly for public ceremonial use, the soft style of gamelan performance developed beyond the type of formal and sparse punctuated choral singing associated with the *bedaya* dance. The soft style carried on the *kemanak* tradition (and maintained this) but never strayed far from its roots in Javanese poetry. More instruments were added, such as the two-stringed *rebab*, the bamboo flute, the wooden-keyed *gambang*, and bronze-keyed *gender*. The most important use of the soft-playing ensemble was to accompany *wayang kulit* performances. Until very recently, the gamelan ensemble used for *wayang* was a small one that did not include instruments such as the *bonang*, which in the loud-style ensembles (Munggang, Kodokngorek, or the sixteenth-century Sekaten gamelans) is the most important melodic instrument.

The bringing together of gamelan instruments from various types of ensembles to form the full modern Javanese gamelan orchestra has taken place only over the last two centuries. As the instruments have come together, so has the music changed and developed. The type of gamelan music we hear today performed on a full modern orchestra is certainly different from what we know of gamelan music even at the end of the nineteenth century, which is the earliest period for which we have any relatively complete records. What gamelan used to sound like in earlier times is still a mystery.

One thing is clear, however. Within gamelan music today, the distinction remains between what we can loosely term 'loud' and 'soft' styles. Central Javanese gamelan music has found its own unique blending of the two. Perhaps one key to appreciating Javanese gamelan lies in being able to understand the relationship between these two styles, for which there are still distinct repertoires. But much of the subtlety and complexity of gamelan lies in the change of focus from the loud to the soft style even within the performance of one piece of music.

2

The Instruments

GAMELAN gets its name from the low Javanese word *gamel*, which refers to a type of hammer, like a blacksmith's hammer. The name 'gamelan' actually refers only to the instruments themselves, which are predominantly percussion. Javanese have a separate word for the art of playing gamelan instruments, namely *karawitan*, a noun formed from the word *rawit*, meaning 'intricate' or 'finely worked'.

In a complete gamelan orchestra there are about twenty different types of instruments. However, the total number of instruments may be as high as seventy-five, as there need to be at least two of most of them, one for each of the two tuning systems. Some instruments (for example, the *kempul*) also exist as a set, and each item of that set may be counted separately.

The Phrase-making Instruments

The *gong, kempul, kenong, ketuk*, and *kempyang* can be called phrase-making instruments and are found in both the loud and soft ensembles.

Gong

The largest phrase of a gamelan melody is marked by the deepest sounding and largest instrument, the large gong or *gong ageng*. There is at least one large gong in each gamelan set, but it is common to have two, and old gamelan sets may have three or more. It is only this large gong that is called *gong* in Javanese. All the other gong-shaped instruments, in the English-language sense of the word, have other names.

The *gong ageng* is made of bronze, as are most of the other instruments of the gamelan, and is on average about 90 centimetres in diameter. It is the most honoured instrument of the

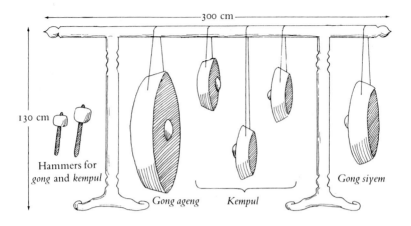

Figure 2. *Gong ageng, kempul, and gong siyem.*

gamelan and the most sacred. Usually the *gong ageng* has its own name (which is often bestowed on the entire set) and it is given an offering of flowers and incense each Thursday night to placate the spirits which are thought to live in and around it.

Another large gong, smaller in size (and thus higher in pitch) than the *gong ageng*, is the *gong suwukan*, which, as it is less resonant than the *gong ageng*, is used when the gong strokes are closer together. Like the *gong ageng*, it is used for the final gong stroke.

The *gong suwukan* is the same size as the *gong siyem* which, unlike the *gong suwukan*, is cast bronze (rather than beaten) and has a particularly resonant sound.

Kempul

The small hanging gong is called the *kempul*. This punctuates a smaller musical phrase than the *kenong*. Like the *kenong*, there was formerly only one *kempul* in a gamelan orchestra, but now there may be as many as ten, one for each note of the two tuning systems. Like the big gong, the *kempul* has a protruding

4. Arrangement of *kempul* and *gong*, Yogyakarta.

5. *Gong/kempul* player, sitting surrounded by the instruments, Yogyakarta.

knob or boss in the centre where it is struck with a soft, padded mallet.

Kenong
The *kenong* is a large kettle gong laid horizontally on crossed cords inside a wooden frame. There was originally only one *kenong* in a gamelan set, and some of the older gamelan sets still have three. However, as gamelan has developed, the number of *kenong* pitches has been extended to include all the notes in two tuning systems.

Ketuk
The *ketuk* is a small, slightly flatter horizontal gong tuned to a certain pitch. It is usually also played by the *kenong* player with the same kind of mallet—a long stick bound with red cord at the end. The sound of the *ketuk* is short and dead compared with the clearer, more resonant tone of the *kenong*. (The

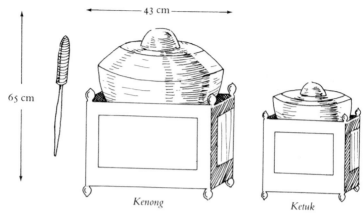

Figure 3. *Kenong* and *ketuk*.

Javanese names of these phrasing instruments are, in fact, onomatopoeic; compare the resonance in the words *gong*, *kempul*, *kenong*, and *ketuk*.)

6. *Kenong* (*slendro* only), Kraton Surakarta.

7. *Kenong*, showing full set of *pelog* and *slendro* kettles. The *kenong* player is striking the *ketuk*, Yogyakarta.

Kempyang

The *kempyang* is a set of two horizontal gongs tuned to almost the same pitch. It is played with one or two mallets like the one used to strike the *kenong*. The *kempyang* works together with the *ketuk*, usually subdividing a *ketuk* phrase. However, whereas the *ketuk* is an essential gamelan instrument, the *kempyang* can often be dispensed with. Sometimes a single musician plays both *ketuk* and *kempyang*, in which case only one of the *kempyang* kettles is struck.

The Loud Instruments

In gamelan performance, the instruments described above mark musical phrases, and therefore may be found in both the loud and soft gamelan ensembles. The instruments in the next group are traditionally instruments of the loud-playing style.

Saron

The basic instrument type is the *saron*, which is a type of metal xylophone or metallophone made of heavy bronze bars laid over a hollow wooden trough, and struck with one wooden hammer. There are three types of *saron*, with an octave interval between each.

The lowest-pitched *saron* is the *saron demung* which is also the largest of the three in size. The middle-register *saron* is called the *saron barung* and the small, high *saron* is called either the *saron peking* or the *saron panerus*. The hammer used to strike this small *saron*, unlike the wooden hammers used to strike the other two *saron*, is made of buffalo horn. It is lighter than the wooden mallets, and produces a more piercing metallic tone. While there may be many *saron demung* and *saron barung* in a complete gamelan orchestra, there is only one *saron peking* (one for each tuning system), for its brilliant tone could easily overshadow the general *saron* tone. Historically, the *saron peking* is a relative newcomer to the gamelan orchestra, and in Yogyakarta at least, there is still no uniformly accepted way of playing it.

8. Arrangement of the three types of *saron* behind the *bonang barung*. The *saron demung* is at the front, the two *saron barung* are behind, and the *saron peking* (without musician) is at the back, Yogyakarta.

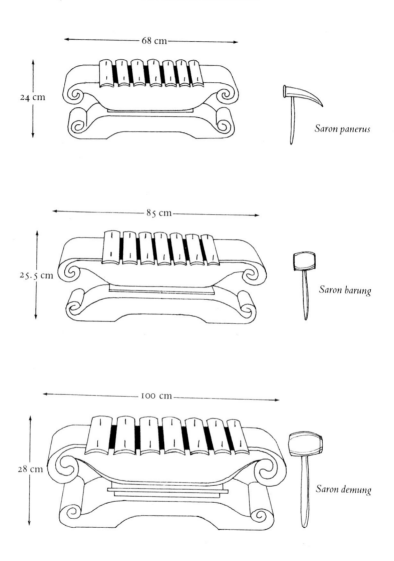

Figure 4. Three types of *saron*.

9. *Saron peking* with its buffalo-horn hammer, Kraton Surakarta.

Bonang

The *bonang* consists of a double row of bronze kettles (like small flat *kenong*) resting on a horizontal frame. There are three kinds of *bonang* in three different octave groupings.

The largest and lowest in pitch, the *bonang panembung*, is now an archaic instrument and is not included in modern gamelan orchestras. The important *bonang* is the middle-sized one, the

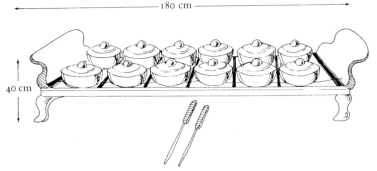

Figure 5. *Bonang barung.*

bonang barung, but the highest in pitch, the *bonang panerus*, has an important function in playing interlocking patterns with the *bonang barung*.

The *bonang* is played with two sticks bound with red cord at the striking end (a smaller version of the *kenong* mallet). It is the most dominant instrument in the loud style of playing, but is usually dispensed with in the pure soft style of playing gamelan music. Although in the modern Javanese gamelan the *bonang* consists of a double row of bronze kettles, originally it had only a single row, as it still does in Bali.

10. Young *bonang* player at class, Solo.

11. *Bonang barung*, Sri Wedari, Solo.

Kendang

The drum is an important leading instrument in Javanese gamelan in both the loud and soft style of playing, in terms of both its tempo and rhythm and its melodic patterns and signals.

The drums in Javanese gamelan are all double-headed, hand-beaten drums, with the exception of the giant drum, the *bedug*, and the drum in the old Munggang gamelan, which are beaten with a drumstick. There are three main sizes of drums, all made from hollowed tree-trunk sections from the jackfruit (*nangka*) tree with cow or goat skin stretched across both ends, and with hide straps to adjust the tightness of the drum heads.

The largest of the three is the *kendang gending*. On its own, this drum is used for soft-style playing, but when combined with the small *penuntung* or *ketipung* drum, the pair lead the loud ensemble and are collectively called *kendang kalih* (literally, 'two drums').

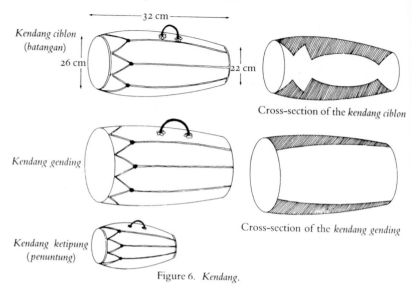

Figure 6. *Kendang*.

The middle-sized *kendang batangan* or *kendang ciblon* is chiefly used to accompany dance and shadow puppet performance. The intricate drum patterns indicate specific dance movements, or movements of the *wayang* puppets. When this drum is played with the gamelan in either loud or soft style and not accompanying dance or *wayang*, the patterns played on it remain the strict dance and *wayang* patterns.

The technique of *kendang ciblon* playing is very difficult to acquire. 'Ciblon' is the Javanese name for a type of water-play, popular in villages, where a group of people, through smacking the water with different hand-shapes, produce complex sounds and rhythmic patterns. These sounds are imitated on the dance drum.

The Soft Instruments

Slentem

The instrument that anchors a basic melody in the soft ensemble, as the *saron* does in the loud ensemble, is called the

12. Playing *kendang kalih*, the *kendang gending* in the front with the small *kendang ketipung* immediately behind. The *kendang ciblon* is on the musician's left, Yogyakarta.

13. The *kendang ciblon*. The drummer is watching the dancer at a dance class, ISI Yogyakarta.

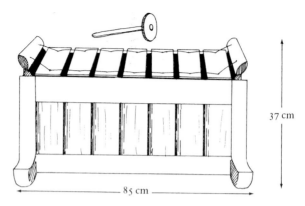

Figure 7. *Slentem*.

slentem. It consists of thin bronze bars suspended over bamboo (or now more often tin) resonating tubes. It is struck with one padded disc on the end of a stick. The register of the *slentem*, which is the same register as the *kenong*, is an octave lower than the *saron demung*.

14. *Slentem* in the front, with *gender barung* behind, Yogyakarta.

Gender

The shape of the *gender* is similar to the *slentem*'s but the *gender* has thirteen keys to the *slentem*'s seven and it covers over two octaves. The *gender* is played with two hammers of the *slentem* disc type but smaller in size. The player's hands act as dampers (as with the *slentem*), but as the *gender* is played with two hands, each hand must simultaneously hit one note and damp the

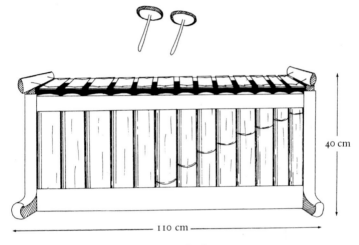

40 cm

110 cm

Figure 8. *Gender.*

preceding one. Both the technique and musical knowledge involved in playing the *gender* well are very demanding, and therefore the *gender* is considered to be one of the finest instruments of the gamelan ensemble.

Like the *bonang* and the *saron*, the *gender* has a 'younger brother', the *gender panerus*, which is tuned an octave higher.

Gambang

The *gambang* is the only gamelan instrument with keys not made of bronze. Instead, the keys, which can cover over three octaves, are made of hard wood, usually ironwood, commonly used for railway sleepers. These keys are laid over a wooden

15. *Gambang*, Kraton Surakarta.

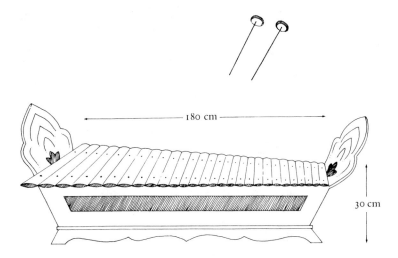

Figure 9. *Gambang.*

trough frame and struck with two long sticks made of supple buffalo horn, each ending with a small, round, padded disc. Unlike the *gender* keys, the wooden keys of the *gambang* do not need to be damped.

Celempung and Siter

The *celempung* is a plucked zither. It usually has twenty-six strings arranged in thirteen pairs, each pair tuned to the same pitch (as on a mandolin). The strings are stretched over a slightly raised wooden trough resonator, and are plucked with the thumbnails. As retuning the *celempung* is a tedious business, there are usually two instruments in a full gamelan ensemble, one tuned to *slendro* and one to *pelog*.

The *siter* is a smaller version of the *celempung* with fewer strings, and an octave higher in pitch. The body of the *siter* is box-shaped and many *siter* can be inverted; the strings on one side are tuned to *slendro* and on the other tuned to *pelog*.

16. *Celempung*, Kraton Yogyakarta.

17. Close-up of *celempung* (and *siter*) technique.

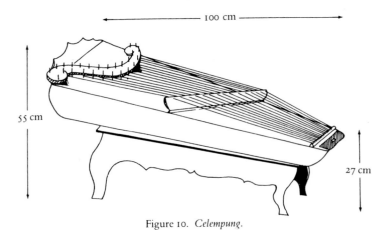

Figure 10. *Celempung.*

Suling

The *suling* or flute is the only wind instrument in the gamelan orchestra. It is made of bamboo and played vertically. There are two *suling*, one for each *slendro* and *pelog* tuning systems.

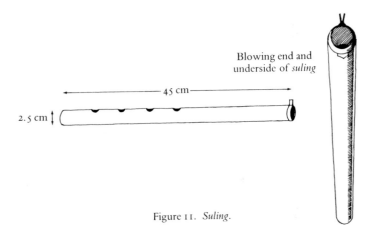

Blowing end and underside of *suling*

Figure 11. *Suling.*

Rebab

The *rebab* is a two-stringed bowed instrument, whose name is clearly of Arabic origin. Technically described as a 'two-stringed bowed lute', the *rebab* consists of a wooden body (traditionally, but now very rarely, made of a single coconut shell) covered with very fine stretched skin, like a banjo. The moveable bridge is made of finely carved wood. The two strings of brass wire are tuned a fifth apart. The bow of the *rebab* is made of wood and coarse horse hair tied loosely, not stretched tight like the bows of modern Western stringed instruments. Part of the technical difficulty of playing the *rebab* involves controlling the correct tension of the hairs of the bow with one's right hand.

The *rebab*, both technically and in terms of the breadth of musical knowledge its performance requires, is a very difficult

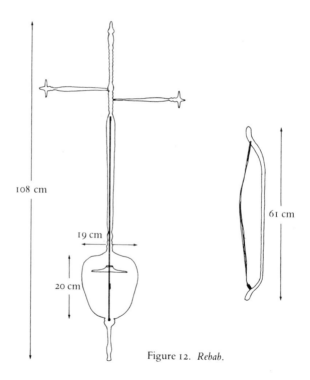

108 cm

19 cm

20 cm

61 cm

Figure 12. *Rebab*.

instrument to play, and its function in the gamelan orchestra as melodic leader and as a bridge between voice and other instruments is an extremely important one. *Rebab* players sit cross-legged on the floor, and stand their instruments on the ground in front of them. There are usually two *rebab* in a set of gamelan instruments, one for *slendro* and one for *pelog*; but these are never played simultaneously.

Singing

The last 'instrument' of the soft ensemble to be considered is the singing, which can be divided into the male singing, called *gerongan*, and the female singing, called *sindenan*. The male singers (*gerong*) sing together as a group, and sometimes some of the instrumental players sing along too. The female singing-line is (except for one style accompanying the court dance *bedaya*) always solo.

Unlike the Western concert tradition where traditionally the function of the orchestra is to accompany the voice, in the Javanese gamelan orchestra the singing is no more or less important than any other instrument; its function is yet another

18. *Gerong* chorus, Kraton Yogyakarta.

19. *Pesinden*, recording session, informal dress, Kraton Surakarta.

20. Dancer at Kraton Yogyakarta with *pesinden* in formal dress.

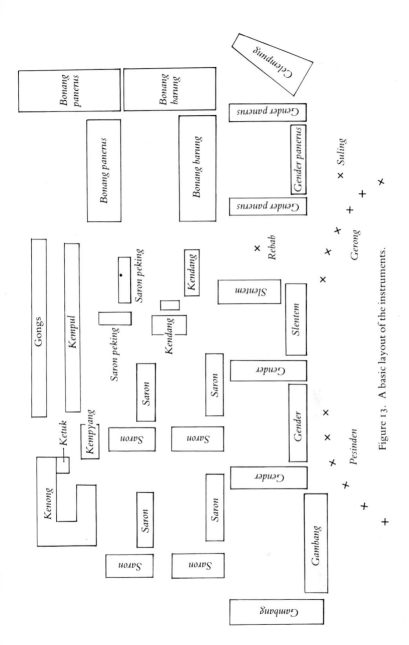

Figure 13. A basic layout of the instruments.

21. Overhead view showing general arrangement of gamelan instruments. While the actual arrangement varies, the general principle is that loud instruments are at the back, elaborating instruments towards the front, and *kendang* near the centre, Yogyakarta.

34

22. *Kendang* player joins singing *gerongan*, Yogyakarta.

melodic layer in the overall structure of the music. A piece of gamelan music is usually complete when the singing is present, but it is possible, and quite satisfying musically, to play the same piece without it.

The Making of the Instruments

The bronze gamelan instruments are made from a mixture of tin and copper; three parts tin to ten parts copper. The word for 'gamelan' in high Javanese is *gangsa*, a word in common Javanese etymology supposed to be formed from the two words *tembaga* (copper) and *rejasa* (tin), or from the numbers *tiga* (three) and *sedasa* (ten) expressing their proportions.

The process of making gamelan instruments is arduous and exacting. The instrument-maker himself will supervise the measuring of the tin and copper mixture. Then his assistants will be called in to help with the melting down process. After the molten metal has been poured into the moulds and allowed to cool, the hammering begins. For this work, only a few specialized assistants will participate.

35

If a bronze key (as for a *saron* or *gender*) is to be made, the mould is smaller than the final size of the key. The key is then hammered until it approximates, but is still higher than the desired pitch. The chief instrument maker will probably do the final tuning, filing the key until it is smooth and in tune. Finally, the two holes for the support nails are bored through the bronze bar. They must be bored at the correct place or the tuning and quality will be affected.

The instruments that are kettle-shaped, like the *bonang* or *kenong*, are also beaten into shape, not moulded. The molten metal is poured to make a small, round disc. Three to five beaters then hammer this disc, hammering from the middle out. When the wall is shaped, the 'bowl' is set on a rock mould with a knob in the centre, and hammered on to this mould. In this way the knob (*pencu*) is formed. In a similar process, the great Javanese gongs, renowned the world over for their resonance and richness of tone, are made.

In Java today there are said to remain only two gongsmiths, or *pande*, who have the technical and spiritual knowledge to make a gong 90 centimetres or more in diameter. The process, though basically the same as making the smaller *kenong*, is on a much bigger scale, and the chances of something going wrong are therefore also much greater.

On the day that the metal for the gong is to be poured, the gongsmith and his assistants meditate to seek success for the project, and make offerings to any spirits who might otherwise disturb them in their work. The offering is simple, for example, a pile of cooked rice in the shape of a gong, and a banana to signify the yellow colour of the finished bronze gong. The gongsmith meditates to ask guidance for the choice of the right anvil to be used when beating the gong into shape.

During the course of about one month, the gongsmith and his assistants beat into shape the small bronze disc, initially about the size of a dinner plate, each time hammering only for fifteen seconds before reheating the metal. Inside the smithy it is quite dark, and it is important that this be so, for then the red metal is more visible and it is easier to determine the thin and thick areas of the disc as the disc is heated. The beaters beat the glowing disc alternately as the turner turns the disc evenly between each group of strikes. Then the disc is returned to the heat again, with the man working the bellows fanning the fire until the disc again glows bright red. And so the rhythm continues until the gong is made. If at the end of this long process the gong is good, of correct pitch and a deep, even resonant sound, the gong can be sold for up to US$2,000. If the workers are unlucky, the gong will not 'sound' and they must melt it down and begin all over again.

Making a complete gamelan set is obviously a long procedure. Bamboo resonating tubes must be exactly matched for the pitch of the *slentem* and *gender* keys, and frames for all the instruments must be intricately carved and painted.

23. Gilt painting on frames, Yogyakarta.

3
Tuning and Notation

Tuning

In Javanese gamelan there are two tuning systems, one of five tones, called *slendro*, and one of seven tones, called *pelog*. A complete gamelan orchestra has both tuning systems. The five-toned *slendro* is said by the Javanese to be the older of the two tuning systems, a natural development from an archaic three-toned scale.

There are two common explanations given for the word *slendro*. The first is that it derived from Sailendra, the name of the family that ruled in central Java in the eighth to ninth centuries and during whose reign the great temple of Borobudur was built. The other, more mythical, explanation attributes greater antiquity to *slendro*, namely, that the five-toned tuning system was given to the Javanese much earlier by the god Sang Hyang Hendra.

The seven-toned *pelog* is said to be a more recent development, deliberately fashioned to sound different from *slendro*, and to express different feelings. One explanation given for the name *pelog* is that it is a variant of the Javanese word *pelag*, meaning 'fine' or 'beautiful'.

The Javanese feeling for the relative antiquity of *slendro* is demonstrated in the fact that this tuning system is the one reserved for use in those shadow puppet plays that depict the *Ramayana* and *Mahabharata* epics, while *pelog* is used for performances of the more recent indigenous Javanese stories, such as the *Panji* cycle. In Bali, too, *slendro* is considered to be the older of the two systems, and is reserved for the shadow puppet performances.

The main difference between *slendro* and *pelog*, however, is not in the number of tones in the tuning systems, but in the intervals between the tones. *Slendro* is made up of five equal, or relatively equal, intervals; that is, the intervals between the notes are roughly equal (around $1\frac{1}{4}$ tones each). *Pelog*, however, is made up of unequal intervals of short and large steps; the small interval is about the same as a Western diatonic semitone or half-step, while the large interval is almost a minor third. In the performance of compositions in *pelog*, only very rarely are all the seven tones sounded; rather, the pitches of this tuning system are divided into two scales that represent a combination of five out of the total seven tones. In effect, then, Javanese gamelan uses three five-tone or pentatonic scales.

The *slendro* tuning system can be shown in Western notation as follows:

The *pelog* tuning system can be shown as follows:

The *pelog* 'subdivisions' can be shown as follows:

Slendro and *pelog* are said to express different feelings. *Slendro* is said to express deep happiness or deep sadness, and also the feeling of *semedot*, which means 'drama' or 'tension', as when a rope is pulled taut. *Pelog*, on the other hand, is said to be more majestic. *Pelog bem* (*patet lima, patet nem*) is said to be noble and calm and to convey a sense of majesty. It also conveys the feeling of detachment necessary for meditation. *Pelog barang* is more emotional, conveying feelings of sadness (but not of profound sadness) and *trenyuh*, which means 'moved' or 'touched' as when one feels great tenderness in love.

The two tuning systems, *slendro* and *pelog*, each contain three modes called *patet*. In *slendro*, these are called *patet nem, patet sanga*, and *patet manyura*. In *pelog*, they are called *patet lima, patet nem*, and *patet barang*. In Javanese, the word *patet* means 'to restrain'. Musically, *patet* refers to a subdivision of the tones of *slendro* or *pelog* into three groups, very much like modes in medieval Western music, each group differing from the others in the way the notes are treated musically. Each group, or *patet*, will consist of five tones, but these tones are given different hierarchical prominence in each of the *patet*. *Patet* is therefore a limitation on the player's choice of variation, so that while in one *patet* a certain note may be prominent, in another it must be avoided, or used only for special effect. Awareness of such limitations, and exploration of variation within them reflects a basic philosophical aim of gamelan music, and indeed all art in central Java, namely, the restraint and refinement of one's own behaviour.

In the shadow puppet theatre, the three *patet* are each related to a different period of the performance. The *patet* are distinguished from each other both in terms of time over an all-night performance (where *patet nem* corresponds to the period 9 p.m. to around 1 a.m.; *patet sanga*, 1 a.m. to around 3.30 a.m., and *patet manyura*, 3.30 a.m. until dawn) and in terms of dramatic structure, where in the performance itself the three *patet* contrast in their proportion of action, narration, and dialogue. Extramusical associations such as this are also part of the musician's

1. Gamelan Munggang, named Kyai Guntur Laut, Kraton Yogyakarta.

2. Obsolete instruments, *byong* (left) and *rojeh* (right), from the Kodokngorek gamelan ensemble.

3. *Kendang bedug*, which is hit with a drumstick, Kraton Yogyakarta. The *bedug* is used in the Sekaten gamelan and also for certain gamelan compositions, particularly to accompany male combat dances.

4. Two *gong ageng*, Kraton Yogyakarta.

5. *Kenong* player at women's gamelan class, Yogyakarta.

6. *Bonang* student, STSI Solo.

8. *Suling* player, RRI, Yogyakarta.

7. *Gambang* student, STSI Solo.

9. *Rebab* student, STSI Solo.

10. At the smithy: filing a *saron* key (left), polishing a *bonang* kettle (centre), and filing a *kempul* (right).

11. Beating a *bonang* kettle into shape.

12. An iron gong, just completed, being tested for tuning and sound quality.

14. Checking the tuning of a *saron* key against the *slentem*.

13. Tuning a *saron* key.

16. Carving the frames.

15. Carving the outside of a *kendang ciblon*.

17. Painting the frames.

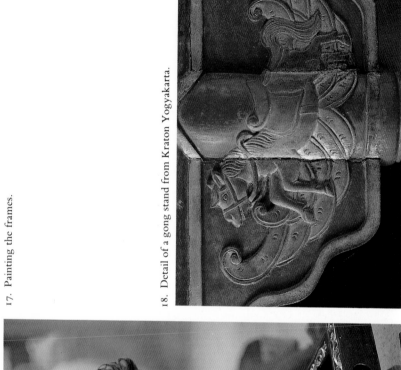

18. Detail of a gong stand from Kraton Yogyakarta.

19. *Wayang kulit*, Yogyakarta.

20. *Gender* player accompanying *wayang kulit*, Yogyakarta.

21. Practice session for a women's gamelan group, Yogyakarta.

22. Dance class, ISI Yogyakarta.

23. Gamelan class, STSI Solo.

24. Children's gamelan class, Solo.

understanding and musical rendition of *patet* when playing instrumental music.

The representations of the *slendro* and *pelog* tuning systems in Western notation shown above should not be regarded in any sense as absolute. Not only is it difficult to convey non-Western scales with Western notation, but also because, in general, no two gamelan sets will have exactly the same tuning, either in pitch or in interval structure. There are no Javanese standard forms of these two tuning systems.

There are two reasons for this. The first reason is historical, for Javanese tradition ruled that the ancient, sacred gamelan sets could not be copied exactly. The same ruling applied (and to some extent still applies) to the tunings of the palace gamelans. Even today it is considered impudent and something of an insult to an old, revered gamelan set for someone ordering a new gamelan to deliberately copy exactly the older tuning. The tuning of a gamelan set must be understood as part of its own identity, together with the actual sound quality of the bronze itself. In the same way, as Western concert musicians seek out the special quality of, say, a Stradivarius violin, so too does a Javanese musician appreciate the individual tone and tuning of a particular set of gamelan instruments.

There is another reason, though, why the Javanese tuning systems have not been standardized, and this reason is closely related to the first. Javanese musicians understand and appreciate the advantages of subtle differences in tuning in the performance of gamelan music. Expert musicians will know which pieces of music sound best on which gamelan sets, and which gamelan sets sound happy, sad, or majestic, for example. This is not merely a question of pitch, but an aspect of the intervallic structure of the tuning of each gamelan set, so that different sets will favour the tuning of different *patet*. Certain *patet* divisions will sound clearer on one gamelan set than another, so that one *slendro* gamelan may be particularly expressive in *patet sanga*, while another may sound better in *patet manyura*. This does not mean that the other *patet* sound out of tune; they merely sound slightly different. Variation of tuning is a Javanese aesthetic to be desired. Distinctions between what is 'in tune' and 'out of tune' are extremely subtle and different to the way a Western musician may apply them.

Finally, though, we must also acknowledge the difficulty in tuning gamelan instruments. The bronze instruments require filing to change their tuning. This is difficult work, and to tune an entire gamelan set is a long process. A new gamelan set takes at least twenty years to settle in its tuning, and the high cost of tuning a gamelan is a strong disincentive to the owner to keep the tuning exact.

For many reasons, then, the Javanese both appreciate and tolerate a much greater deviation from a sensed 'normal' tuning than Westerners would.

Notation

Notation does not play the important part in gamelan music that it does in Western music. First, musicians do not learn to play through reading notation, nor do they usually use notation in performance. Secondly, even when gamelan music is notated, it is done so in only skeletal fashion, and the musician uses this notation merely as a basic melodic line from which his or her performance is generated.

Traditionally, Javanese musicians learnt to play by ear, beginning on the instruments that are easier technically and graduating to the more difficult instruments as their knowledge of repertoire and technique developed. Notation did not play a part in this process, and indeed it was only in the late nineteenth century that any system of notation for Javanese gamelan developed, not as a system for use in performance but for the sake of keeping written records of gamelan repertoire, especially in the palace libraries.

The palaces and princely houses of Yogyakarta and Surakarta developed various systems of notation. In each instance the basic concept was the same, namely, to notate the musical line played on the *saron* and *slentem* and to indicate with sparse musical markings both the phrasing instruments and the melodic contours of the singing and soft-style elaborating instruments.

A very early system of notation in Yogyakarta consisted of writing out in full the names of the *slendro* and *pelog* notes as played on the *saron*. In *slendro* and *pelog*, the tones have names that refer to their degree in the tuning system expressed in terms of the human body.

They are, from low to high:

panunggul   head   ⎫ (forming the torso, or basic physical
gulu   neck   ⎬ structure)
dada   chest   ⎭

lima   five; the five senses: sight, smell, touch, taste, hearing

enem   six; the Javanese sixth sense or *rasa*, meaning 'perception' or 'feeling'; a spiritual sense.

The two extra notes in the *pelog* tuning system are *pelog*, the fourth note (meaning 'fine, beautiful') and *barang* (meaning 'unidentified thing'). The seven *pelog* tones are then: *panunggul, gulu, dada, pelog, lima, enem,* and *barang*.

In Yogyakarta, the system that was developed in the palace over the early twentieth century discarded the cumbersome system of notating the names of the notes and replaced them with abstract symbols. This system is known as chequered notation, and is similar in concept to Western notation except that the lines run vertically, not horizontally:

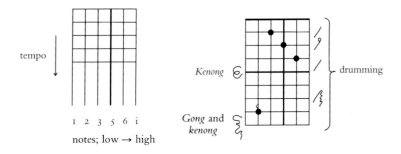

tempo

notes; low → high

Kenong

Gong and *kenong*

drumming

For *slendro* there are six vertical lines, one for each of the five
tones, plus the upper octave of the first tone. The line for the
fourth tone is printed darker than the others to facilitate reading
the notation. The horizontal lines mark the rhythmic beats and
the dark lines (every fourth) act as a type of barline, which are
marked by the punctuating instruments. The round black dots
represent the notes themselves, moving always from the top
towards the bottom of the page. The symbols on the left of the
stave are the symbols for the punctuating instruments (*ketuk*,
kenong, *kempul*, *gong*), while the symbols on the right are
indications for the drumming.

In Surakarta, the notation systems developed used the same
principle, but the stave lines were written horizontally, as in
Western notation. This system is not as clear to read because
the tempo is not marked with even lines and barlines. Instead,
the beat is indicated by squiggly lines between the notes:

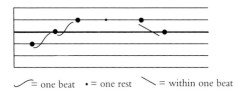

= one beat   • = one rest   = within one beat

In the late nineteenth and early twentieth centuries, another
'reference system' of notation was developed by Javanese gamelan musicians as a way of keeping track of the extensive
gamelan repertoire. In this system, the notes of *slendro* and *pelog*
are assigned numbers, just as in Western notation the notes are
referred to by the letters A, B, C, D, E, F, and G. The cipher
system is often referred to as 'Kepatihan notation', as it is said
to have developed in the residence of the *patih* or prime
minister of the court of the Surakarta *kraton*.

In the cipher system, the tone names in *pelog* correspond with numbers as follows:

LOW ——————→ HIGH

panunggul	gulu	dada	pelog	lima	enem	barang
↓	↓	↓	↓	↓	↓	↓
1	2	3	4	5	6	7
↓	↓	↓	↓	↓	↓	↓
head	neck	chest	'fine'	five	six	'thing'

In *slendro*, because the words *lima* (five) and *enem* (six) already named the fourth and fifth tones (counting from low to high), the number four was left out so that the numbers would then correspond to the names:

LOW ——————→ HIGH

panunggul (barang)	gulu	dada	lima	enem
↓	↓	↓	↓	↓
1	2	3	5	6
↓	↓	↓	↓	↓
head	neck	chest	five	six

The use of numbers means that staves (lines) do not need to be used at all, and the music can be written very concisely:

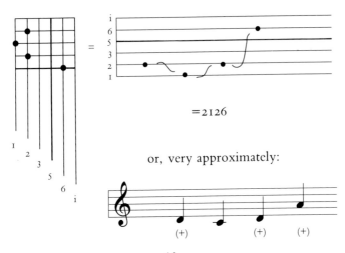

= 2126

or, very approximately:

45

The disadvantage of this system is that it is not as comprehensive as its skeletal predecessors. There is no indication of the drumming, and only minimal indication of the general melodic movement of the music. High notes are represented with a dot above the cipher ($\dot{2}$), and low notes with a note below the cipher ($\underset{.}{2}$). Rhythmic patterns such as syncopation can also only be suggested with simple symbols such as a single or double line above a note to indicate subdivisions of a beat:

$\overline{66}$ 6

and pauses are represented with a dot.

6 6 . 6

Nevertheless, the Kepatihan notation is now used extensively in Java, and the older systems are found only in palace records.

4
The Structure of Gamelan Music

Background

THERE are three basic concepts that are crucial to understanding the way that Javanese gamelan music is structured, namely, the polyphonic layering of melodic lines, the cyclic structure of the music, and the ability of the melodic lines to expand and contract.

In understanding the melodic layering of sound, it is useful to start with the basic distinction between monophonic and polyphonic music. Monophonic music is music that has only one part, or various voices of the same part in different octaves. Polyphonic music has two or more parts moving individually. Javanese gamelan is highly polyphonic, with as many as twenty different parts playing together.

The way these parts play together, however, is different to the interrelationship of parts in Western music as we know it today. In some ways, gamelan music resembles a much more complex system of the way Western music used to be structured in the late sixteenth century before the development of harmony, when one musical part (usually the tenor) held a basic melody with other parts carrying interrelated melodic lines that moved independently but always worked towards common pauses, when all the parts converged.

Layering

In gamelan music it is a general principle that the larger and lower in pitch the instrument, the more infrequent are the notes (or beats) played on that instrument. The higher in pitch the instrument, the faster that instrument plays and the more notes it plays in relationship to the others. The music is made up of a proportionate layering of sound, from the largest and most resonant of the instruments, the *gong*, to the instruments playing filigree-like elaborations of sound, like the *gender panerus* or the *siter*. The music that you hear is made up of many layers of melody all overlapping and interlocking to form one whole.

One way of understanding this layering is to dissect the music, showing each layer in isolation. For example, if each 'dot' represents one musical beat, we can start with the time-keepers, the *ketuk* (t) and *kempyang* (p), which may play together in one pattern, as follows:

```
 .   .   .   .   .   .   .   .
 t   p   t   ·   t   p   t   ·
```

The *kenong* (N) is then added at the end of this line, marking one *kenong* phrase:

```
 t   p   t   ·   t   p   t   N
```

The *kenong* phrase is subdivided by the *kempul* (P):

```
 t   p   t   P   t   p   t   N
```

This full *kenong* phrase, with its internal subdivisions of *ketuk*, *kempyang*, and *kempul*, may be repeated four times before the *gong* beat, which will coincide with the fourth *kenong*. The *gong* marks one cycle that will then be repeated in form, although the notes may differ. The *gong* marks the end of the largest musical phrase, much like the end of a large verse of poetry. It is a culmination of all that has gone before, and the big gong, which has every gamelan note in its rich overtones, has the fullness of an ending chord in Western music.

To this underlying structure we can now add the *saron* and *slentem*, which will usually play one note to each of the beats shown above. The part that the *saron* and *slentem* play is called the *balungan*, and is the only line that is notated. *Balungan* means 'skeleton' (*balung* = bone) and the line the *saron* and *slentem* plays is just that—a mere skeleton that cannot exist alone, but must be filled inside and fattened on the outside by the other instruments. For example, a *balungan* line that is phrased by the above phrasing structure could be as follows:

```
2   1   2   6   2   1   6   5
p   t   p   ·   p   t   p   N

6   5   2   1   3   2   1   6
p   t   p   P   p   t   p   N

2   3   2   1   6   5   2   1
p   t   p   P   p   t   p   N

3   2   1   6   2   1   6   5
p   t   p   P   p   t   p   N
                        GONG
```

The other instruments of the gamelan all play more notes than the *saron* and *slentem*. Some of them play patterns that are very close to the *saron* line, doubling or quadrupling this in various ways, either anticipating or following the *saron*. For example, the *bonang* and the *saron panerus* could play the first line of the above pattern like this:

```
saron                2   1   2   6   2   1   6   5
saron panerus        2 2 1 1 2 2 6 6 2 2 1 1 6 6 5 5
bonang               2 1 2 . 2 6 2 . 2 1 2 . 6 5 6 .
```

or like this:

```
saron panerus        2211221122665566221122116655665 5
bonang               212. 212. 262. 262. 212. 212. 656. 656.
```

Other instruments, such as the *gender*, *gambang*, or *celempung*, also elaborate upon the basic line, but their part is much more loosely attached to it. The parts played on these instruments are in no way mere mathematical rhythmic subdivisions of the *saron* line. Rather, the *gender* or *gambang* player must think in longer musical phrases, usually working towards a *kenong* phrase and taking account, particularly, of the melodic contour of the singing-line and the *patet* of the composition. The part played on these instruments leaves more room for individual improvisation by the musicians. Different *gender* and *gambang* musicians will interpret the melodic phrases differently, depending both on their technical skill and the depth of their knowledge of the whole piece, for example, their knowledge of the singing-line. The complexities and variations of these lines make them too difficult to represent here in notation.

The drum acts as the rhythmic leader of the gamelan ensemble, marking the tempo changes. However, the patterns on the drum are also particular to each form of gamelan composition. The form just shown above, for example, is called a *ladrang*. A *ladrang* has four *kenong* phrases to one *gong* phrase, with the *kenong* phrases subdivided by the *kempul*, which is in turn subdivided by the *ketuk* and *kempyang*. But there are many other forms, and another form will have a different alignment of these instruments and a different drum pattern. It is primarily the drum pattern that signals the differences in form. A good gamelan musician can identify the musical form immediately from the drum signal that commences during the melodic introduction to a piece.

Once the drummer plays on the dance drum, or *kendang ciblon*, however, the drum strokes are less tightly tied to the form of the composition. The patterns played in the dance drum are patterns of dance movements that must be linked together following rules of dance sequence, which in turn relate to the overall phrasing of the gamelan.

While the drum is the rhythmic leader and defines the form in gamelan, the *rebab* is the melodic leader. The *rebab*, like the *gender*, *gambang*, and *celempung*, is also an elaborating instrument, but its melodic line is much closer to the singing, as it is only the *rebab* and the singers that are not limited to fixed pitches. In fact, the *rebab* acts as a kind of bridge or interpreter between the singing and the other instrumental parts. Like the *gender* or *gambang* player, the *rebab* player also thinks in large musical phrases, usually marked by a *kenong*, but he or she weaves around these phrases, sometimes delaying, sometimes anticipating the overall melodic contour, and always conscious of the *patet* of the composition. The *rebab* is considered by gamelan musicians to be the most difficult of all the instruments to play, for apart from the extensive musical knowledge required, it also requires mastery of a difficult technique. The *rebab* line is often punctuated at the end of a phrase by the flute.

The singing is, in a sense, the top layer of all the melodic layering in gamelan music. The female singing part, *sindenan*, is, like the *rebab*, less tied rhythmically to the other instruments. Individual singers have their own styles of syncopation, pausing, and phrasing. The tone quality of the voice is nasal, blending in timbre with the *rebab*. The nasal tone means that the singing is distinguishable in the overall sound but is not dominant—at least it should not be dominant. (An unfortunate modern tendency is to amplify the *sindenan* part, which destroys the traditional balance of the music.) The female singing part weaves around the male chorus, the *gerongan*, which is less florid and more rhythmically tied to the *balungan* than the *sindenan* line.

The texts sung by the singers are taken from Javanese poetry. Only very rarely are there specific set texts for specific pieces of gamelan music. The sung melodic line is in no way a 'song' set to music. Rather, a singer can choose any text that has the correct poetic structure to fit with the musical phrasing of the piece being performed. Different poetic forms are defined in terms of their rhyming patterns (for example, the vowel sound at the end of the line) and the number of syllables per line. A singer, after choosing the appropriate poetic form, must then match the phrasing of the poetry with the musical phrasing.

In practice, there is a certain number of 'favourite' texts that are interchanged from one gamelan composition to another. The content of these texts varies. It could be a love poem, or perhaps an extract from a classical text. It may be just a linguistic riddle involving a witty play on words, or it could be a moral lesson, like this one:

Yen wong anom anom iku
Kang kanggo ing mangsa iki
Andap asor kang den simpar

Ambeg gumunggung ing diri
Obrol umuk kang den gulang
Kumentus lawan kumaki.

which freely translated is:

Young people
In this day and age
Do not care about using humble, refined speech
Are vain, and always seeking praise.
Their speech is arrogant and practised.
They are boastful and like showing off.

This particular poetic form is called *kinanti*, which has an end-of-line rhyming scheme of u/i/a/i/a/i. The *kinanti* form is unusual in Javanese poetry as its six lines all have the same number of syllables—eight. This even division gives the *kinanti* form great versatility when it is aligned with the gamelan and it is thus the poetic form most frequently used.

The alignment of the poetic form *kinanti* with the musical form *ladrang* is as follows:

```
 .   .   . t   .   .   .   .     .   . . t   .   .   . N
 .   .   . t   .   .   . P       .   .   . t   .   .   . N
        8 syllables 'u'                 8 syllables 'i'

 .   .   . t   .   .   . P       .   .   . t   .   .   . N
        8 syllables 'a'                 8 syllables 'i'

 .   .   . t   .   .   . P       .   .   . t   .   .   . N/G
        8 syllables 'a'                 8 syllables 'i'
```

Cyclic Structure

Just as Javanese poetry is written in verses, each verse leading on to the next, only changing form at the end of a canto, so too does a gamelan composition consist of repeated cycles of gong phrases, but one composition with its repeated verses can lead on to another musical form to make a larger unit, or medley, in performance. Within one composition, a gong cycle may be played a number of times, the actual number in performance depending on the drummer. The singer will usually choose a new poetic verse for each time the musical verse is played, although it is also quite common to repeat the text. The phenomenon of repeated cycles, rather than a single linear progression of a piece of music from the beginning to the end, is a basic characteristic of gamelan music.

Expansion and Contraction

Another important characteristic of gamelan music is the phenomenon of expansion and contraction. In very simplified form, this refers to the proportion of notes played on the *saron* and *slentem* in relation to the number of notes played on the elaborating instruments. The Javanese term for this relationship, and for the changes in this relationship through contraction and expansion, is *irama*.

Irama refers to the proportionate distribution of notes of the *saron* line (the *balungan*) to all the instruments that play more notes than this line. The faster the *saron* line is played, the closer the *saron* notes are together, and the less time for filling in by the other instruments. The slower the *saron* line, the further apart the *saron* notes become, and the more opportunity there is for the doubling and quadrupling filling-in by the elaborating instruments. There are four *irama* in Javanese gamelan, but not all gamelan compositions can be played in all four *irama*.

To take the example of the *saron panerus*, it will play two notes to each note of the *saron* in *irama I*, four notes to one on the *saron* in *irama II*, double this to eight in *irama III*, and in *irama IV* it will double this again to sixteen.

saron				X					X		
saron panerus											
irama I				X		X		X		X	
irama II		X	X	X	X	X	X	X	X		
irama III	X	X	X	X	X	X	X	X	X	X	X	X	X	X	X	X
irama IV	XXXXXXXXXXXXXXXXXXXXXXXXXXXXXXXXX										

When the drum slows the *saron* line down, the *irama* can change. The *saron* will then be playing half as fast, and the elaborating instruments begin to 'fill in' the musical spaces between the *saron* notes. As the *saron* line slows down again, the elaborating instruments can double their time. The *saron* line can thus expand to include different levels of elaboration, or contract to restrict such elaboration.

Most gamelan compositions can be played in more than one *irama*, and usually in at least two or three. The style of performance is also closely linked to *irama*. In general terms, the faster the *irama* (that is, the faster the *saron* line), the louder the piece of music, as the soft elaborating instruments will drop out and the focus of the music will shift to the loud instruments, like the *saron* and the phrasing instruments. Usually there is no singing once the *irama* of a piece is fast. Conversely, the slower the *irama* (the slower the *saron* line is played), the more opportunity there is for the soft-style elaborating instruments and singers to join in.

The division of *irama* shows one important way in which the loud and soft style of performance can exist within a single gamelan piece. One gamelan piece can be played many different ways. When the *irama* is fast, the loud instruments are in the foreground, but when the *irama* slows down, these instruments move to the background, and the soft instruments predominate. Like a piece of cloth woven in two different colours, the same piece of music can be heard in different ways at different times. Part of the enjoyment of listening to Javanese gamelan music is hearing the foreground and background interchange in this way.

In simple terms, the repertoire of Javanese gamelan consists of pieces which are only or predominantly loud style, pieces which are predominantly or only soft style, and pieces which freely move from one to the other. Often the loud-style pieces have closer phrasing, with the *gong*, *kenong*, and *kempul* strokes closer together, but there are also extremely long and majestic compositions in pure loud style, featuring the *bonang*, with no singing or soft instruments. Similarly, whereas the soft-style compositions are usually made up of longer *kenong* and *gong* phrases, this is not always the case.

Whether loud or soft style, the music can be seen as an elaborate layering, with the *saron* and *slentem* at a middle level, and all other instruments playing either a denser line (more notes) or fewer notes than this. Or, another way to look at it, is to see the layering of the music as a continuous process of phrasing, working from the singing-line and *rebab* phrases answered by the *gender* and *gambang*, whose phrases are in turn answered by the *bonang*, and so on all down the line—or upwards to the apex, depending on which way you look at it, to the *gong*.

The very fine and elaborate structuring of layers in sound in gamelan music reflects the ordered structuring of Javanese society. As with Javanese language and etiquette, the complex interrelationships are designed to minimize the unpredictable. Every note played on each instrument has been so thoroughly prepared for, so thoroughly led towards, that it has become inevitable. And so, beginning with the singing and moving down the layers, each instrument is answering the phrasing of the preceding layer until we reach the *gong*, which answers all. If the *gong* player forgets to hit the *gong* after all the players have been preparing for it, and when the phrasing so urgently calls for it, the players are visibly disturbed.

A gamelan musician must learn to sense this wholeness of sound and the overall interlocking of phrases, which is also acquired through mastery of an extensive repertoire. The process of learning gamelan is, like all music, a combination of musicianship and technical skill, but with gamelan music it is particularly important that a musician learn to be sensitive to and work within an overall texture of sound. Although the many gamelan instruments have different technical requirements—some very complex, some apparently simple—all of the instruments are equal in importance. Gamelan playing is not a soloist's art; no one melodic line can be singled out and played alone. As with Javanese society, the mark of being a good musician is being able to fit in integrally, indispensably, and unobtrusively with one's neighbours.

5
Gamelan in Javanese Society

THE recent trend in the development of instrumental gamelan music in Java has been, more than anything else, its increasing interdependence with other art forms. Gamelan has always existed in its instrumental form, as well as in its supportive role when combined with dance, *wayang kulit*, or dance drama (*wayang orang*), but the distinction between these roles has become increasingly blurred. Today, gamelan exists both as instrumental music, which incorporates elements of poetry, dance, and *wayang*, and as an integral part of those art forms themselves.

Up until this century, within the central Javanese courts, the repertoire of music for dance and the instrumental repertoire were kept quite separate. Eighteenth- and nineteenth-century court texts, when listing gamelan repertoire, distinguish between gamelan in terms of use; for example, listing separately instrumental gamelan compositions, compositions for *wayang*, and those for dance.

Yet, it is precisely the inclusion of elements from dance that now gives the gamelan its modern style. One of the most important examples of this is the use of the dance drum, the *kendang ciblon*. Prior to the beginning of this century, this dance drum was never used in the palaces, but today it is difficult to imagine Javanese gamelan without it. The patterns played on the dance drum are exact dance patterns. The drummer must follow a strict sequence of patterns that parallel a sequence of dance movements. A dancer could follow these drum patterns and interpret them into movement even if there were no other gamelan instruments playing. A drummer in the gamelan today performs these patterns on the *kendang ciblon* whether or not a dancer is physically present.

Similarly, the *wayang* repertoire has strongly infiltrated instrumental gamelan performance. One example of this is the use of *patetan*, which is a short, rhythmically free interlude played on a few soft instruments to establish a sense of each *patet*. In *wayang kulit*, *patetan* is performed throughout the performance with the puppeteer's (*dalang's*) voice leading the accompaniment by the *rebab*, *gender*, and *gambang*. In instrumental gamelan, *patetan* is usually performed without any voice, but it is also common for one of the other musicians to sing the *dalang's* part.

The gamelan repertoire for *wayang kulit* has a special level of flexibility in expanding and contracting. This is because the music must be able to react quickly to changes of movement on the screen, and so there is a whole body of music for *wayang* that has irregular, but frequent, gong phrases, and is able to speed up, slow down, stop, and start at a moment's notice. This repertoire, too, is now an integral part of both instrumental gamelan and gamelan music for dance.

24. The *dalang* (with microphone) sits behind the screen in a *wayang kulit* performance, Yogyakarta.

25. Gamelan musicians sit immediately behind the *dalang* in *wayang kulit*, Yogyakarta.

59

Wayang itself would be impossible to perform without game-lan. The gamelan is in no sense mere musical accompaniment, but it is a completely integral part of the performance. The *dalang*'s narration, for example, is structured in delivery and pitched to the gamelan. The puppets come to life with the subtle and varied drum patterns that make them move. Certain kingdoms and characters in *wayang kulit* have certain gamelan compositions specifically associated with them, and the per-formance of these pieces sets the scene and names the character. There is not one moment in the *wayang* when there is no musical element of the performance. In the same way, the form of dance drama known as *wayang orang*, which can be described as *wayang kulit* performed by people rather than puppets, is also framed musically by the gamelan.

Javanese poetry is also integrally linked to gamelan, as it is to *wayang* and dance, and this link has become stronger in the performance of instrumental gamelan over the past eighty

26. *Wayang orang*, Sri Wedari, Solo.

27. Gamelan musicians accompanying *wayang orang* from the pit, Sri Wedari, Solo.

years. All Javanese poetry is sung. There is no tradition of poetry written to be read without melody 'in one's head'. If a text written in poetic form is 'read', then it must be read aloud as song. Usually, there is no musical accompaniment for this. There are many different melodic forms for each different poetic form, and the reader can choose which melody to use. In the late nineteenth and early twentieth centuries in Yogyakarta and Surakarta, dance forms were developed that used these poetic forms (called *macapat*) but added gamelan accompaniment, which added a level of rhythmic restriction to the singing. This style of singing verse (called *palaran* or *rambangan*) is still very popular, long after the dance forms that developed them have virtually died out, and it is common for sections of *palaran* singing to be inserted into instrumental gamelan performance.

While the repertoires and styles of playing instrumental gamelan, dance, and *wayang* used to be more separate and different than they are today, it is interesting that of these, it was only gamelan that had no separate audience of its own, that is, an audience for music alone. Even today, gamelan music is something one does rather than something one listens to—unless, that is, it is accompanying dance or *wayang*. There is no 'concert tradition' for gamelan music in Java. In the courts, gamelan accompanied *wayang* and dance when an audience would usually be present, but instrumental gamelan was used as background music for special occasions, or as ceremonial music when the pieces performed were determined by the ceremony. Outside the courts, too, the idea of people sitting in a large group to listen quietly and attentively to the performance of gamelan was and is a strange notion.

Gamelan for gamelan's sake is musician's music. It is something musicians do to get together. The very way that the music is structured encourages this, for it is unsatisfying to play any gamelan instrument alone. In order to learn to play, one must play with other people. There is no point in locking oneself away in a room to practise technique for hours alone. Rather, a gamelan student will find other people to play with, for the learning is not only how to play, but what to play, and what one plays depends on what other people play and on being aware of the larger phrasing of the whole gamelan ensemble.

A gamelan musician learns to play by finding other people to play with. A person wishing to learn will start with one of the technically more simple instruments, usually the *saron*, as there are several *saron* playing an identical melody, making it easier to follow along, and mistakes will not be too obstrusive (unlike on the *kenong* or *gong*). The process of learning is a process of absorbing knowledge about form, melody, and technique. While it is possible to start with a more simple instrument and a more simple gamelan form, there is always a more difficult level to attain. Over time the musician moves to learn different instruments, until ideally he or she has mastered at least the basics of them all, and is constantly learning more complex repertoire.

Because of gamelan's initial 'playability', it is accessible to a wide spectrum of society. There used to be many amateur neighbourhood or village gamelan groups, but they now seem to be declining—both in competition with television and because so few neighbourhoods and villages now own sets of instruments. But where gamelan sets are still owned by wealthier Javanese, these people will usually open their houses to their neighbours who want to play. Such sessions will begin in the evening, and the guests will sit, alternately playing, sipping sweet tea, and smoking cigarettes, until eleven or twelve at night. The people who play will be from all kinds of social backgrounds, for the playing of gamelan cuts across formal barriers of class or occupation.

Traditionally, the musicians are male, women joining only for the *sindenan* singing part. In the courts, the one instrument that used to be considered appropriate for a woman to play in a mixed ensemble was the *gender*, as the playing position, with its subtle wrist action, did not require ungraceful movement.

In the villages, women may perform in a gamelan ensemble to accompany the *wayang*, and in fact it used to be common for the *dalang*'s wife to be the *gender* player, although nowadays this is quite rare. Today, although there is technically no taboo on women performing with men, women usually have their own gamelan groups. Most women, however, play gamelan only half seriously and form social clubs which meet in the afternoon or early evening when they can play, chat, and perhaps go in for a bit of harmless trading on the side. In general, though, women with an interest and talent in the performing arts traditionally have been drawn to the more prestigious art of dance rather than gamelan. This is true even today.

Since the mid-1960s, there has been a new phenomenon in the teaching and performance of central Javanese gamelan music, that is, the establishment and blossoming of the tertiary academies for the performing arts in Yogyakarta and Solo. These academies grew as a follow-on from the secondary-level conservatories which were established in the 1950s and still continue to give secondary-level teaching in the traditional performing arts. The tertiary institutions are now known as the

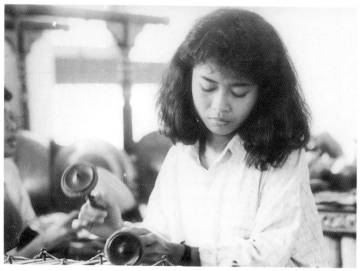

28. *Gender* student at gamelan class, ISI Yogyakarta.

Indonesian Institute of the Arts (or ISI in Yogyakarta) and the Indonesian College of the Arts (or STSI in Solo). Both of these schools also teach Javanese dance and the art of *wayang* performance, apart from gamelan music, and ISI Yogyakarta encompasses visual arts and Western music, too.

These schools are shaping a new identity for gamelan as instrumental music. Their students must face examinations that require them to perform in an orchestra in a concert situation. The teachers are arbiters of style and establish clear standards of what is acceptable and not acceptable in performance of traditional repertoire. Their students must study gamelan theory and are encouraged to compose modern compositions for gamelan. Graduates from these schools are staffing not only these same schools as teachers, but also government offices from which positions they organize competitions for gamelan groups to perform instrumentally, and at which prizes are given for the best group. The schools are training musicians who make up not only the performers but also, perhaps more significantly, a modern audience for instrumental gamelan.

While it is true that there is still no real concert hall audience for gamelan, it does have one other important audience, and this is the audience that buys the very many cassettes of gamelan music and also listens to gamelan on the radio. While it is saddening to see a decline in the number of amateur neighbourhood and village gamelan groups, on the other hand, gamelan seems to be developing a wider listening audience through radio broadcast, but now particularly through cassette recordings. Perhaps some of those people who would, a couple of decades ago, have joined a gamelan group as a hobby are now the people who listen to it more on their cassette recorder or on the radio.

Both recordings of gamelan music and live music are still an integral part of certain Javanese functions, such as wedding receptions or circumcisions. However, the fancier the reception, the more the likelihood that there will be something other than gamelan alone, for example, a traditional dance (usually accompanied by recorded gamelan music) or, if the host is particularly

29. Technicians recording the weekly gamelan broadcast of the radio station's resident gamelan ensemble, RRI, Yogyakarta.

wealthy and wants to show it, a full *wayang kulit* performance.

Javanese gamelan is not, and never has been, the sole prerogative of the courts, nor is it now the sole prerogative of the performing arts institutions, although in both cases they see themselves as setting standards and maintaining the classical tradition. Outside of the courts and academies, however, gamelan exists in a myriad of other forms and instrument combinations. In Yogyakarta, for example, a common form of street music is *siteran*, in which one or more *siter* players will approximate the sound of a more complete gamelan. A small ensemble of gamelan instruments, like *gong*, *kenong*, and *kempul*, can be used to accompany all kinds of village performances, such as trance dances, sometimes together with the *terbang*, a large tambourine-like drum. The range of instrument combinations, performance styles, and uses of gamelan is enormous.

It is hard to avoid concluding, however, that most Javanese do not really revere their gamelan musicians and the enormous skill and knowledge it takes to be a good one. In the courts, the musicians were always the lowest paid of the court artists, their salaries well below that of a dancer or a *dalang*. Even today, it is common for musicians to get paid less than dancers for a performance, and when musicians are asked to perform at a reception, they are usually treated no better than the waiters. There are extremely few opportunities for a good musician to earn decent money, except if a musician is lucky and is invited to teach abroad or has some well-paying private (usually foreign) students. If a musician gets a permanent teaching position in the arts academies, the salary may be regular, but the heavy load of administration and teaching will reduce the opportunities to actually perform.

So why do people learn gamelan? First, because it is fun and continually challenging. But apart from this, like the other Javanese arts, the learning of gamelan is also the art of learning Javanese aesthetics of beauty and restraint, which are part of learning a whole social code of behaviour. A Javanese gamelan master, the late R. Ng. Martopangrawit, in his comprehensive book on gamelan theory, as a kind of final signature to his book, in an acrostic poem that spells out part of his name in the first syllable of each line (Mar-ta-pa-ngra-wit ing Su-ra-kar-ta), wrote about the relationship between the study of gamelan music and its meaning in this way:

Marsudiya kawruh jroning gending
Taberiya nrasakke irama
Pangolahe lan garape
Ngrasakna wosing lagu
Witing patet saka ing ngendi
Ing kono golekana
Surasaning lagu
Rarasen nganti kajiwa
Karya padang narawang nora mblerengi
Tatas nembus Bawana

Practise the inner knowledge of gamelan music.
Patiently learn to sense the rhythm,
The structure and the working out of the variations.
Understand the basic content of the melody
And the restraint of *patet*, where that is from.
There you can search for
The expression of the melody.
Ponder this until your soul
Becomes clear, unblemished, unblurred
Transcending to pure peace.

Notes on Spelling and Pronunciation

IN Javanese, there are two different sounds for each of the letters 't' and 'd'. One form is dental, with the tip of the tongue touching the back of the top teeth, the other is formed by curling the tip of the tongue back to the alveolar ridge. In the writing of Javanese words in roman script, these differences are not always shown. If they are shown, they are represented as follows:

    d: dental d

    ḍ or dh: alveolar d

    t: dental t

    ṭ or th: alveolar t

Similarly, Javanese has three different forms of 'e' which are not represented when Javanese is written in roman script. They are as follows:

    é: as in bait (*pande*)

    è: as in bet (*cara balen*)

    ĕ: as in bird (*gending*)

In the body of the text of this book, for the sake of readability, these differences have not been shown. However, in the Glossary that follows, all alveolar 'd' and 't' are also shown as 'dh' and 'th' and the 'é' and 'è' are differentiated with accent markings.

Vowels: i: as in beet (*irama*)

            u: as in boot (*talu*) or bull (*bedug*)

            o: as in bought (American) or hot (British) (e.g. *saron*); or as in boat (*slendro*)

            a: as in artist (*saron*) or as in hot (*tembaga*)

Consonants: as in English except:

            c: as in English *ch*in or Italian *c*iao

            r: a rolled r

Glossary

Balungan.   Skeleton; skeletal melodic outline.

Barang.   Name of a tone in the *pelog* and *slendro* tuning systems. *Patet barang* is the name of one of three *patet* in *pelog*.

Bedaya/Bedhaya.   Female court dance.

Bonang.   Set of small kettle gongs suspended horizontally over a wooden frame.

Bonang barung.   Middle register *bonang*.

Bonang panembung.   Lower register *bonang*.

Bonang panerus.   High register *bonang*.

Celempung.   Large zither with 22–26 strings.

Dada/Dhadha.   'Chest'; third tone (lower to higher) of the *slendro* and *pelog* tuning systems.

Dalang/Dhalang.   Master performer of *wayang kulit*; puppeteer.

Enem.   Six, tone 6, 'sixth sense'; name of the fifth tone (lower to higher) in the *slendro* and sixth tone (lower to higher) in the *pelog* tuning systems. See also *Nem*.

Gambang.   Wooden-keyed multi-octave xylophone.

Gamel.   Hammer.

Gangsa.   High Javanese word for 'gamelan'.

Gendèr.   Instrument with thin metal keys suspended over tuned tube resonators.

Gendèr panerus.   High register *gender*.

Gending/Gendhing.   Piece of music or composition for gamelan.

Gérong.   Male chorus.

Gérongan.   Vocal part sung by the male chorus.

Gong ageng.   Largest gong in a gamelan orchestra.

Gong siyem.   A medium-sized gong of cast bronze.

Gong suwukan.   A medium-sized gong of beaten bronze.

Gulu.   'Neck'; name of the second tone (lower to higher) of both the *slendro* and *pelog* tuning systems. (High Javanese word is *jangga*.)

Irama.   Rhythmic subdivision in gamelan; level of subdivision of the *balungan* beat.

Karawitan.   Gamelan music (from *rawit*, meaning 'finely worked').

Kemanak.   Bronze banana-shaped gamelan instrument, held in the hand.

Kempul. Small hanging gong.

Kempyang. Small kettle gong suspended horizontally.

Kendang/Kendhang. Side-ended drum.

Kendang batangan/Kendhang batangan. Yogyakarta term for dance drum; see *Kendang ciblon.*

Kendang ciblon/Kendhang ciblon. Dance drum.

Kendang gending/Kendhang gendhing. Largest *kendang.*

Kendang kalih/Kendhang kalih. Set of two drums, the *kendang gending* and the *kendang ketipung.*

Kendang ketipung/Kendhang ketipung. Smallest drum.

Kenong. Large kettle gong suspended horizontally.

Kepatihan. Residence of the prime minister (*patih*); Javanese system of cipher notation said to have been first developed at the Kapatihan in Solo.

Ketuk/Kethuk. Small kettle gong suspended horizontally.

Kinanti. One six-line form of *macapat* Javanese poetry, the form often used for *gerongan* texts.

Kodokngorèk/Kodhok Ngorèk. Name of piece of music played on archaic gamelan set, now commonly used to name the gamelan set itself.

Kraton. Palace of the Sultan (Yogyakarta) or Sunan (Surakarta).

Ladrang. One *gending* form in gamelan music.

Lima. 'Five', tone 5; fourth tone (lower to higher) in the *slendro* scale; fifth tone (lower to higher) in the *pelog* scale. *Patet lima* is the name of one of the three *patet* in the *pelog* tuning system.

Lokananta. Name given to a mythical prototype gamelan set.

Macapat. Sung poetry in modern Javanese, for which there are many forms differing in melody, rhyme pattern, number of syllables per line, and number of lines.

Manyura (Patet manyura). One of the three *patet* in the *slendro* tuning system.

Munggang. Name of a three-toned archaic gamelan ensemble.

Nem (see also Enem). Six, tone 6; also as *Patet nem*, one of the three *patet* in the *slendro* tuning system.

Palaran. *Macapat* poetry accompanied by a few gamelan instruments.

Pandé. Smith, especially a gongsmith.

Panunggul. First tone in the *pelog* and *slendro* tuning systems; lowest tone.

Patet/Pathet. To limit; modal subdivision of *pelog* and *slendro* tuning systems.

Patetan/Pathetan. Introductory setting of the musical *patet*, played by the *gender*, *gambang*, and *rebab*; poetic sections sung by the puppeteer in shadow puppet performance.

Pélog. Tuning system of Javanese gamelan with seven uneven intervals to the octave.

Pencu. Knob.

Pesindèn/Pesindhèn. Female singer.

Rambangan. As for *palaran*, Yogyakarta style.

Rasa. Feeling/thinking, perception.

Rebab. Two-stringed bowed lute.

Rejasa. Tin.

Sanga (Patet sanga). Name of one of the three *patet* in the *slendro* tuning system.

Saron. Single-octave metallophone with keys suspended over a trough resonator.

Saron barung. Middle register *saron*.

Saron demung. Lower register *saron*.

Saron panerus. Higher register *saron* (also called *Saron peking*).

Saron peking. See *Saron panerus*.

Sekatèn. Name of the Muslim Holy Week in Java; also the name of the archaic gamelan ensembles played for ceremonies throughout this week.

Sindènan/Sindhènan. Vocal part sung by the female chorus.

Siter. Small zither with 10–26 strings.

Sléndro. Tuning system of Javanese gamelan with five roughly equidistant intervals to the octave.

Slentem/Slenthem. Instrument with thin bronze keys suspended over a tube resonator; also called the *Gender panembung*.

Suling. End-blown bamboo flute.

Tembaga. Copper.

Terbang. Frame drum; large tambourine-like drum.

Wayang kulit. Traditional shadow puppet theatre.

Wayang orang. Form of dance drama based on *wayang kulit*.

Suggested Further Reading

THIS brief list of further reading is intended as a basic guide only. For ease of reference, the list is linked to the subject divisions of the chapters of this book.

The most comprehensive bibliography of Javanese gamelan is:

Heins, Ernst (1989), *Music in Java: Current Bibliography 1973–1989*, Amsterdam: Universiteit van Amsterdam. Ethnomusicologisch Centrum 'Jaap Kunst'.

For those who do not read Indonesian or Javanese, the study of Javanese gamelan by non-Javanese has at last been placed in a more balanced context with the publication in English translation of invaluable source material written by Javanese musicians and scholars. See Becker, Judith and Feinstein, Alan, eds. (1984, 1987, and 1988), *Karawitan: Source Readings in Javanese Gamelan and Vocal Music*, 3 vols., Ann Arbor: University of Michigan, Center for South and Southeast Asian Studies.

The Historical Background

Fontein, Jan (1990), *The Sculpture of Indonesia*, Washington: National Gallery of Art. (Written as an extended catalogue to the 'Classic Art of Indonesia' exhibition, which was curated for the Festival of Indonesia in the United States in 1991, this book contains an excellent general introduction to Javanese prehistory and early history.)

Holt, Claire (1967), *Art in Indonesia: Continuities and Change*, Ithaca: Cornell University Press. (Still the most comprehensive book on Indonesian arts, with detailed sections on Javanese performing arts, particularly dance and dance drama.)

Kunst, Jaap (1973), *Music in Java: Its History, Its Theory, and Its Technique*, 2 vols., 3rd rev. edn., E. L. Heins, ed., The Hague: Martinus Nijhoff. (Earlier English edition 1949; first published as *De Toonkunst van Java*, 1934). (The most comprehensive study of Javanese gamelan music ever written. The early chapters contain a survey of writing about the history of gamelan instruments, tuning, and performance in Java. Vol. 2 contains photographs and a full bibliography, which has been updated by Heins (*Music in Java*).)

Ricklefs, M. C. (1981), *A History of Modern Indonesia*, London and Basingstoke: The Macmillan Press Ltd. (Contains a good introduction to Javanese history in the context of Indonesian history.)

The Instruments

Kunst, *Music in Java*, Vol. 2, contains good photographs of gamelan instruments, including many from the late nineteenth century.

Toth, Andrew (1975), 'The Manufacture of Gongs in Semarang', in *Indonesia*, 19: 127–72. (This is a translation, with an introduction, of 'De Gong-Fabricatie te Semarang' by Edward Jacobson and J. H. van Hasselt (1907), Rijks Ethnographisch Museum Serie II, No. 15, Leiden: E. J. Brill.)

Tuning and Notation

Becker, Judith (1980), *Traditional Music in Modern Java: Gamelan in a Changing Society*, Honolulu: University of Hawaii Press.

Hood, Mantle (1966), 'Slendro and Pelog Redefined', in *Selected Reports*, 1: 28–48, Institute of Ethnomusicology, University of California.

Kunst (*Music in Java*) devotes a great portion of his book to the discussion of Javanese tuning systems and theories of the development of these tuning systems, reflecting the major preoccupation of musicologists in the 1920s and 1930s when this book was written. Kunst also provides detailed information on notation for gamelan, and in particular the chequered notation from Yogyakarta which was perhaps seen to be more important in the 1930s than it has proved to be since that time.

Powers, Harold S. (1980), 'Mode', in *The New Grove Dictionary of Music and Musicians*, 6th edn., 10: 376–450. (Powers' entry on mode contains a detailed discussion of *patet*.)

The Structure of Gamelan Music

Becker, Judith (1979), 'Time and Tune in Java', in A. L. Becker and Aram A. Yengoyan, eds., *The Imagination of Reality: Essays in Southeast Asian Coherence Systems*, Norwood: Ablex Publishing Corporation.

(An excellent essay discussing the cyclic structure of gamelan music and relating this to other notions of cyclical structure in Javanese society.)

Hood, Mantle (1958), *Javanese Gamelan in the World of Music*, Yogyakarta: Kedaulatan Rakyat. (This essay was published as a small pamphlet. Hood discusses the layering of Javanese gamelan music, comparing this to early Western music with the layering of organum. The same comparison has been made by many other writers since, but Hood's essay remains an excellent preliminary exposition.)

Martopangrawit (1972), 'Catatan-Catatan Pengetahuan Karawitan', in Judith Becker and Alan Feinstein, eds., *Karawitan: Source Readings in Javanese Gamelan and Vocal Music*, 3 vols., Ann Arbor: University of Michigan, Center for South and Southeast Asian Studies, Vol. I, pp. 1–244. (This is an English translation of an early edition of Martopangrawit's manual of gamelan theory, *Pengetahuan Karawitan*, republished in 1984. It covers in depth the broad subject of structure in Javanese gamelan music.)

Gamelan in Javanese Society

Becker, *Traditional Music in Modern Java*. (Becker discusses modern developments in Javanese gamelan. Written in the 1970s.)

Becker, A. L. (1979), 'Text-building, Epistemology, and Aesthetics in Javanese Shadow Theatre', in *The Imagination of Reality: Essays in Southeast Asian Coherence Systems*, Norwood: Ablex Publishing Corporation.

Holt, *Art in Indonesia*. (Holt's observations on Javanese dance and dance theatre remain fresh today.)

Hood, Mantle (1963), 'The Enduring Tradition: Music and Wayang in Java and Bali', in R. T. McVey, ed., *Indonesia*, New Haven, pp. 438–71, 555–60.

Keeler, Ward (1975), 'Musical Encounter in Java and Bali', in *Indonesia*, 19: 85–126.

Sutton, R. Anderson (1991), *Traditions of Gamelan Music in Java: Musical Pluralism and Regional Identity*, Cambridge: Cambridge University Press. (The first study of regional traditions of Javanese gamelan music. Sutton also discusses the role of the tertiary institutions for the arts, particularly the teaching of gamelan music today in Java.)

List of Gamelan Recordings

READERS are referred to a good selective discography of recordings on vinyl disc and cassette tape of various styles of Javanese gamelan music in Sutton, *Traditions of Gamelan Music in Java*, pp. 273–80.

A full discography of the cassette recordings of the Indonesian recording company LOKONANTA, which produces a large number of Javanese gamelan recordings, has recently been published:

Yampolsky, Philip (1987), *Lokonanta: A Discography of the National Recording Company of Indonesia, 1957–1985*, Bibliography Series, No. 10, Madison: University of Wisconsin, Center for Southeast Asian Studies.

Visitors to Java will find that cassette recordings of Javanese gamelan music are readily available. Those recorded under the label LOKONANTA are of fairly uniform reasonable quality. Many other labels are pirate versions, often of extremely poor recording quality.

There have been many recordings of Javanese gamelan released internationally on vinyl disc. Some of the more readily available are listed here:

Javanese Court Gamelan from the Pura Paku Alaman, Jogjakarta, K. R. T. Wasitodipuro, Director. Nonesuch Explorer Series H-72044;

Javanese Court Gamelan, Vol. II, recorded at the Istana Mangku-negaran, Surakarta. Nonesuch Explorer Series H-72074;

Javanese Court Gamelan, Vol. III, recorded at the Kraton Yogyakarta. Nonesuch Explorer Series H-72083;

Java: Historic Gamelan, Unesco Collection, Musical Sources, Art Music from Southeast Asia Series, IX-2. Philips 6586 004;

Gamelans from the Sultan's Palace in Jogjakarta: Musical Traditions in Asia, Archiv 2723-017 (2 discs);

Java: Langen Wandra Wanara, Musiques traditionnelles vivantes, Ocora 558.507/9 (3 discs);

Street Music of Central Java, Lyrichord stereo LLST 7310.